AGING WELL

THE AGING CHALLENGE

PETER MENCONI

MT. SAGE PUBLISHING

Mt. Sage Publishing
Centennial, CO 80122

TABLE OF CONTENTS

SESSION 1: The New Aging   11

SESSION 2: Longevity Revolution   19

SESSION 3: Denial of Aging   27

SESSION 4: Healthy Aging 1:
              Physically and Financially   35

SESSION 5: Healthy Aging 2: Emotionally   43

SESSION 6: Healthy Aging 3: Spiritually   51

ABOUT THE CASA NETWORK

In 1983, three Southern California churches established the CASA Network ministry to serve their 50+ members through cooperative efforts. The first jointly sponsored one day event was called Jamboree (now Life Celebration). The response to this first event led to a three day retreat held at a Christian conference center. A committee representing various churches met the next year to discover how to meet the growing needs of the Christian adult senior community and to discuss incorporating. They determined that the name of the new organization would be called CASA, Christian Association of Senior Adults.

In 1993 the CASA Board of Directors caught the vision to broaden its ministry to mid and post career age men and women nationally and internationally. In the fall of 1994, CASA launched two quarterly publications – The Energizer for senior adults and Energizing Leaders for leaders of Adults 50+ in the local church. With the explosion of the Boomer generation, a third quarterly publication was launched in 2001 for this population, called Legacy Living. For a time, CASA engaged in a website partnership with Christianity Today.

From 1993 through 1998 regional leadership training conferences were offered to pastors and lay leaders of adult 50+ ministries in a number of states and Canada. In 1998, the first National Leadership Training Conference was held in Irvine, CA and brought together over 300 pastors and lay leaders from 26 states and Canada. A further development in the growth of CASA's ministry was the establishment of a website **www.gocasa.org** that provides resources and information on 50+ ministry. Serving leaders across the country, the CASA Network offers regional, national, and international 50+ leadership conferences. You can access the CASA Network website at **www.gocasa.org** for the latest information on training offerings.

Today, the CASA Network is a premier training and equipping source for the Church's ministry to midlife and beyond age men and women. Augmented by internet and print media, the CASA Network brings together an array of leaders within the field of 50+ ministry to inspire and equip the Church for ministry to and through adults in life's second half. Only God knows how many lives have been touched, how many churches have been changed, how many leaders have been trained because of the vision and leadership of the CASA Network. Check us out at **www.gocasa.org** and welcome to the CASA Network Aging Well Bible Study Series.

BEFORE YOU BEGIN!
Instructions on how to get the most out of this book.

The primary purpose of this Bible study is to help you take a fresh look at aging, reevaluate your current situation, and consider making some changes.

This book contains six Bible study sessions on the topic of aging that can be done individually or in a small group. The studies are written for people who have never studied the Bible, occasionally study the Bible, or often study the Bible. That is, virtually everyone interested in aging will benefit from these studies. Each session allows the Bible to speak to where you are and where God may want you to go.

While these studies can be done individually, they are primarily designed to be done in a small group setting. In fact, you will receive maximum benefit when the studies are discussed in a group. The more diverse your group is in age and experience, the more you will learn from these studies.

SUGGESTIONS ON FORMING A GROUP

1. Form a group that has between eight and 15 members. Groups larger or smaller are generally less effective.

2. One person should be appointed as the group facilitator. The facilitator's primary role is to get everyone together at an appointed time and place. The facilitator also gets the study started and keeps it going without getting off track. After the initial meeting the facilitator role can rotate within the group.

3. At the first meeting have the group members introduce themselves to one another and have each person share his or her responses to the following questions:

a) Where were you born and raised?

b) Where were you and what were you doing at age 10? Age 18? Age 25?

c) What one person, place, or experience has had the greatest impact on your life and why?

4. Before starting the study group members should agree on the length and frequency of meeting times. Normally, each study should take about one hour. All group members should commit themselves to attending all group sessions, unless there are circumstances beyond their control.

5. Give time for the small group to gel. Don't expect everything to click in the first session or two.

Because the interaction in a small group can reach into personal areas, it is important that group members agree upon "ground rules."

SUGGESTED GROUND RULES FOR SMALL GROUP STUDY

1. Jesus said that "the Holy Spirit, whom the Father will send in my name, will teach you all things and will remind you of everything I said to you." With this in mind, each group session should open in prayer asking the Holy Spirit to teach and guide. (Not everyone needs to pray. If a person is uncomfortable praying in public, he or she should be given freedom to remain silent.)

2. No one or two persons should dominate the discussion time. All group members should have an equal opportunity to express their thoughts, feelings, and experiences.

3. Because people's experiences and perspectives vary, there will be ideas, thoughts, and feelings expressed which will be quite diverse. All members should respect one another's perspective.

4. Confidentiality on what is said in the study should be agreed upon by all group members.

5. If significant conflict arises between specific group members, they should make every effort to resolve this conflict apart from group time. That is, they should agree to meet together at another time to discuss their differences.

6. If the group ends in prayer, members should pray for one another.

SESSION 1 | THE NEW AGING

INTRODUCTION
Have one or more group members read the introduction aloud.

The Issue: In what ways has aging changed and how should we respond?

Aging is changing...and changing quite quickly. Most of us have heard or read the amusing proclamations that 50 is the new 30 or 70 is the new 50. We have seen the rapid growth of the anti-aging movement that attempts to reduce and reverse the effects of aging. Each year billions of dollars are spent on dietary supplements, plastic surgery, botox, anti-aging exercises, hair implants and coloring, skin products, hormone therapies and many other treatments as maturing adults chase the fountain of youth.

This new aging is characterized by several major changes that will impact all members of our society, no matter how young or old. The first major change is "the new longevity." Today people are living longer and the percentage of older adults in our society is growing rapidly. While living longer, older adults are also staying healthier. Many will choose to retire retirement and stay in the game by continuing to work or start a new career. Other will balance meaningful involvements, such as volunteerism, with leisure. Still others will realize that they cannot afford to retire and will have to find resourceful ways to support themselves.

A second major difference created by the new aging is the growing varieties of lifestyle alternatives becoming available to older adults. The traditional move to the Sunbelt will become more part-time for many retirees as they choose to stay near kids and grandkids. Others will move to 55+ communities where grandchildren visits are sometimes discouraged. Ranch style homes will increase in demand. Other older adults will move to city centers to take advantage of cultural amenities. Many will choose to age in place as opposed to moving to a senior facility. Still others will move in with their children and grandchildren to create multigenerational households.

And nursing homes will become the last resort for those in failing health.

Another reality of the new aging is that many older adults will find themselves sandwiched between their children and their parents. That is, they may find themselves providing care and assistance for two or three other generations. While caring for aging parents, older adults may also be helping to raise and care for their children and/or grandchildren. Contemporary families have become more complex and aging parents are often the glue that holds them together.

Still another major change of the new aging is that there is greater diversity among older adults. Many more individuals are aging as singles, either never having married or through the loss of a spouse by death or divorce. In addition, the new aging population is less white and more ethnically diverse. And sadly, healthcare costs and financial stress may create a population of older adults that is divided into the haves and have-nots more than ever before.

The changes brought on by the new aging have profound implications, not only for individuals and society, but also for our churches. Today, many churches are aging and in decline. Others struggle as a significant decline in financial giving changes the ways ministry is done. Ministries to older adults are often the first areas to feel the financial cutbacks.

But the new aging of a church also affords ministry opportunities. Older adults have more time and are often looking for meaningful ways to use it. Volunteer and service opportunities are the most obvious, but there are also many creative ways for older adults to invest in ministry. Mentoring, coaching, surrogate grandparenting, business-as-ministry, and short-term mission trips are just a few of the ways older adults can be engaged in ministry and service.

YOUR TAKE

Read and respond to each of the following questions. Discuss your responses with your group.

1. What changes, if any, are you seeing in the way people today are aging?

___ Many older people are in denial of the fact that they are aging.

___ Many older people act like they will stay forever young.

___ Many people believe the myth that 50 is the new 30 and 70 is the new 50.

___ Many people are living longer and staying healthier.

___ Many older people do not know how to spend their time wisely.

___ Many older people are looking for ways to stay in the game.

___ Many people are working beyond the traditional retirement years.

___ There are significant generational differences in the way people age.

___ There is a built-in ageism in our society that discriminates against older adults.

___ Plastic surgery, botox, hair dye and other make-me-look-younger products are a growth industry.

___ Attitudes toward aging have changed little in the past 50 years.

___ Longer life spans have thrown some older adults into a tailspin.

___ Longer life spans have given older adults more opportunities.

___ Longer life spans have given older adults more challenges.

2. As you age, which of the following questions cause you the greatest concern and why?

___ Will my money hold out?

___ What will I do with all my time?

__ Will I stay healthy enough to be independent?

__ Will I be able to age in place or need to go a nursing home?

__ Will I end up being a burden to my family/children?

__ Will I be put out to pasture and be of little use?

__ Will I be able to be a positive influence on my grandchildren?

__ Should I/we relocate to a warmer climate?

__ Will I suffer as I continue to age?

__ Will I leave a positive legacy?

__ Am I ready to meet God?

__ Am I afraid to die?

YOUR REFLECTION

Read the following passages from the Bible and answer the questions that follow.

The glory of young men is their strength, gray hair the splendor of the old.
—Proverbs 20:29

1. What do you think the writer of Proverbs meant by this verse?

2. Do you view gray hair and aging positively or negatively? Please explain your answer.

Do not cast me away when I am old; do not forsake me when my strength is gone
—Psalms 71:9

3. Do you identify with the psalmist in feeling cast aside or ignored? If so, why? Give some examples of how you have been ignored or cast aside.

Since my youth, O God, you have taught me, and to this day I declare your marvelous deeds. Even when I am old and gray, do not forsake me, O God, till I declare your power to the next generation, your might to all who are to come.
—Psalms 71: 17-18

4. These verses indicate that we have a spiritual role to play in our older age. What is that role?

Even to your old age and gray hairs I am he, I am he who will sustain you. I have made you and I will carry you; I will sustain you and I will rescue you.
— Isaiah 46:4

5. In this verse, what promises does God make to us in our old age?

6. How do these promises make you feel?

YOUR APPLICATION

During the coming week, act on the following ways you can better understand and reflect on your own aging process.

1. Reminisce and reflect on how your aging process compares to the aging of your parents and grandparents. In what ways is it similar and dissimilar?

2. Go to a local shopping mall or busy airport. Sit down and observe the people. What do you notice about the older adults there? Does your time of observation and reflection of older adults encourage or discourage you? Explain.

3. From your observations of other aging adults, what changes might you want to make?

SESSION 2 | LONGEVITY REVOLUTION

INTRODUCTION

Have one or more group members read the introduction aloud.

The Issue: As people live longer, how will we, our society, and churches adjust?

If your community is typical, it is aging as Americans are living longer. During the 20th century life expectancy in the United States grew by about 30 years and continues to grow. Today, as people live longer, the number of older adults is growing rapidly. In fact, the 100-plus population is the fastest growing age group with the 85+ being the second fastest. We will soon see the population of older adults outnumbering the population of children.

There are numerous reasons for this increased longevity. Clean drinking water, universal sanitation, improved nutrition, vaccinations, better trauma care, and improved drugs, especially antibiotics, are some of the major reasons. The new longevity is not just about living longer; it's also about living better and maintaining a balanced, vital lifestyle.

Not only does the new longevity have important implications for older adults, but it also will impact the ways all Americans will live their lives. There is a very good chance that young people who are in their 20s and 30s today will live to be 90 or 100. This new longevity will change their whole life cycle and plan. How will their finances sustain this longevity? How will their families be affected? Will they have multiple careers that stretch well beyond traditional retirement years? How will healthcare look? We already see some of these changes brought on by longevity impacting older adults.

Researchers are beginning to identify one major trend that could reverse the new longevity. It is obesity. According to the Center for Disease Control, more than one-third of adults and almost 17% of youth are obese. (It is projected that 43% of Americans will be obese by 2030.) Obesity-related conditions include heart disease, stroke, type 2 diabetes and certain types of cancer, some of the leading causes of preventable, premature death. Might this trend present a ministry opportunity for local churches?

It is becoming obvious that with the increase in life expectancy comes new opportunities and new potential problems. Many older adults can now look forward to additional years, not only for leisure, but also for making a difference in their families, communities, and society. More years also brings new challenges. There are the financial challenges of supporting themselves, and perhaps their kids and parents. Healthcare is a significant challenge for many older adults, both in staying healthy and in paying for medical care. Issues like aging-in-place, moving to a warmer climate, moving near grandkids, moving into a nursing facility, giving and receiving care, and many other complex decisions can complicate aging.

As the age wave continues to flow through our society, followers of Jesus Christ and local churches have a unique opportunity to get creative. As we age we have a choice. We can either become curmudgeons who curse the darkness and the way things are changing or we can become sages who joyfully light the way for others as we seek to apply the good news to a broken world. Living with the new longevity will take some extra effort, but it is effort well invested in God's kingdom.

YOUR TAKE

Read and respond to the following questions. Discuss your responses with your group.

1. Which one of the following statements best expresses your view of longevity and long life?

___ Long life is a gift from God.

___ Long life only prolongs our agony.

___ Long life makes life more complicated.

___ Long life is a burden for others.

___ Long life gives us more of an opportunity to serve God.

___ Long life is a scary thought.

___ Other _____.

2. What has been your experience with a family member or friend who has lived a long life?

YOUR REFLECTION

Read the following passages from the Bible and answer the questions that follow.

The fear of the LORD adds length to life, but the years of the wicked are cut short.
—Proverbs 10:27

1. What does the expression "the fear of the Lord" mean to you?

2. Do you think there is a relationship between righteous living and long life? Please explain your response.

The fear of the LORD is the beginning of wisdom, and knowledge of the Holy One is understanding. For through wisdom your days will be many, and years will be added to your life. If you are wise, your wisdom will reward you; if you are a mocker, you alone will suffer.
—Proverbs 9:10-12

3. Do you think there is a relationship between wisdom and longer life?

4. Can you think of an example, either from your life or the Bible, where unwise behavior has led to a shortened life?

My son, do not forget my teaching, but keep my commands in your heart, for they will prolong your life many years and bring you peace and prosperity.
—Proverbs 3:1-2

"Honor your father and mother"—which is the first commandment with a promise—so that it may go well with you and that you may enjoy long life on the earth.
—Ephesians 6:2-3

5. What advice is God giving to younger people (perhaps our children or grandchildren) in these verses?

6. If you were mentoring or teaching a child or young adult, how would or could you use these verses?

YOUR APPLICATION

The following activities are suggestions on how you can further respond to the subject of longevity during this coming week.

1. In your computer's search engine, type "life expectancy calculator" and choose one of the websites that will project your life expectancy. What do you think of the results?

2. Since we do not know how long we will live, every day is precious and important. What changes do you want to make now that could extend your life expectancy? What changes can you make to improve the quality of your life?

SESSION 3 | DENIAL OF AGING

INTRODUCTION

Have one or more group members read the introduction aloud.

The Issue: Today many people, especially in the Boomer Generation, are in denial of aging. Are you in denial of aging? If so, what can be done to give you a healthy view of aging?

If we live long enough, all of us will get old. This reality does not settle well with many Americans. In fact, Americans are attempting to stay young and ward off aging as never before. We don't have to look very far for evidence. Our supermarkets and pharmacies have shelves filled with anti-aging products that purport to keep us younger from head to toe. As the Boomer Generation ages it has spawned a multi-billion dollar anti-aging industry. Cosmetic surgery and dentistry, Botox injections, hair replacement and testosterone therapies, and many creative youth restoring treatments have become commonplace.

What is behind this powerful desire to deny aging? A major reason is that many people have a negative attitude toward older adults. They see old age as a time of inevitable declining health, social loss, and isolation. In addition, many cannot accept the changes in physical appearance brought on by graying hair, wrinkles, receding hairlines, sagging body parts, decreasing sexuality, and more. The potential for significant memory loss and cognitive ability are other potential downers. Negative attitudes toward aging are further reinforced by thoughts of financial limitations and decreased mobility and freedom. Others simply have an unrealistic fear of growing older. Perhaps they have had bad experiences when their parents aged.

The thought of joining the ranks of older adults can create a denial of aging. Consequently, surveys have shown that most of us feel younger than our chronological age. We see examples of resistance to aging among boomers when they refuse to join the older adult ministry groups in churches or do not join AARP or shun moving into a 55+ community.

Popular perceptions of aging are powerful influences in shaping our attitudes. In our youth oriented culture there are few examples in the media of healthy aging. Most older people are portrayed in TV and movies as forgetful and uninteresting curmudgeons rather than alert, knowing sages. While we are seeing some changes in these depictions, it will be a while before contemporary aging is represented accurately.

As followers of Jesus Christ, how are we to view aging? Where are we to get our guidance on aging? While the Bible doesn't directly address the aging process, it gives some hints on how God views aging. In the Old Testament alone there are over 250 references to old age where it is seen as a blessing or favor from God.

In addition, while wisdom is often attributed to older characters in the Bible, it is not automatically given with advanced age. Instead, it is earned through faithful and righteous living. In Job 12:12 we read, "Is not wisdom found among the aged? Does not long life bring understanding?" We certainly hope so.

In the New Testament older adults also play an important role in the unfolding of the good news. Though advanced in age, Zechariah and Elizabeth conceived their son, John the Baptist, who prepared the way for Jesus Christ. Simeon, an elderly and just man, blessed Jesus and his parents in the temple. The apostle Paul in 1 Timothy 5:1-3 advises young Timothy. "Do not rebuke an older man harshly, but exhort him as if he were your father. Treat younger men as brothers, women as mothers, and younger women as sisters, with absolute purity. Give proper recognition to those widows who are really in need."

In biblical times, it is clear that "elders" were respected and even revered. And they still are in a decreasing number of cultures. Perhaps it is time for followers of Jesus and local churches to reestablish older adults as sages who regularly help guide our young people.

YOUR TAKE

Read and answer each of the following questions. Discuss your responses with your group.

1. On a scale of 0 to 10, with zero meaning "no denial" and 10 meaning "much denial", how do you rate your denial of aging?

0	1	2	3	4	5	6	7	8	9	10

No denial   Much Denial

2. General Douglas MacArthur is quoted as saying, "Nobody grows old by merely living a number of years. People grow old only by deserting their ideals. Years may wrinkle the skin, but to give up interest in life and living wrinkles the soul. Worry, doubt, self-distrust, fear and despair–these are the long, long years that bow the head and turn the growing spirit back to dust."

What is your reaction to this quote? Do you agree or disagree with this quote? Please explain your answer.

YOUR REFLECTION

Read the following passages from the Bible and answer the questions that follow.

There is a time for everything,
and a season for every activity under the heavens:
a time to be born and a time to die,
a time to plant and a time to uproot,
a time to kill and a time to heal,
a time to tear down and a time to build,
a time to weep and a time to laugh,
a time to mourn and a time to dance,

a time to scatter stones and a time to gather them,
a time to embrace and a time to refrain from embracing,
a time to search and a time to give up,
a time to keep and a time to throw away,
a time to tear and a time to mend,
a time to be silent and a time to speak,
a time to love and a time to hate,
a time for war and a time for peace.
—*Ecclesiastes 3:1-8*

Note: The book of Ecclesiastes is a book of protest. It fits well with our issue of the denial and protest of aging. The writer of the book is reflecting on the seasons of life; older age is one of the seasons of life.

1. Do you agree with the statement that "there is a time for everything, and a season for every activity under heaven?" Please explain your answer.

2. Have you experienced different seasons in your life? If so, what have these seasons been like and what have you learned from these seasonal experiences?

3. In denying the aging process, do you think anything is missed? That is, does our aging teach us anything about God and life? If so, what?

4. Do you think there is any connection between the denial of aging and maturing in our relationship with Jesus Christ? If so, how would you describe this connection?

5. If there is a time for everything, what "things" do you think are unique to the time of aging or older adulthood?

YOUR APPLICATION

During this coming week do several of the following activities to give yourself a better understanding of how our culture (and perhaps you) denies aging.

1. Pay close attention to the various media to which you are exposed to see how they treat the aging process. That is, critically listen to and look at TV shows and ads, movies, the internet, print media, radio and music, casual conversations, and other forms of communication to see how the aging process and older age are viewed in our society. Reflect on what you hear and seek to understand how society's views differ from a biblical perspective.

2. Consciously enter into conversations with friends, family members, coworkers, and others about aging and the denial of aging in our society. Make it an enjoyable exercise that gives you the opportunity to hear what others think. Again, reflect on what you hear.

3. Is your view of aging shaped more by our society or by a biblical perspective?

SESSION **4** | HEALTHY AGING 1:
PHYSICALLY AND
FINANCIALLY

INTRODUCTION
Have one or more group members read the introduction aloud.

The Issue: As we age, how do we stay physically and financially healthy?

Two of the major questions that reoccur as we age are "will I stay healthy?" and "will my money hold out?" Concerning the first question, there are obvious ways you can decrease the onset of serious illnesses. Most of us can quote them from memory. Don't smoke or use tobacco products; keep your weight under control; eat healthy foods; exercise regularly; get enough sleep; use alcohol in moderation or not at all; minimize stress; maintain healthy relationships; keep your blood pressure under control; and get regular check ups. These preventive measures give us considerable control over our health as we age.

In recent years much of the research on healthy aging has centered on the aging brain. New research is shattering old thoughts and "facts" about the aging brain. It was thought that the brain could not grow new brain cells and that older adults could not learn as well as young people. Recent research has found that new brain cells form throughout life and that the brain is continually resculpting itself in response to new experiences and learning. It has also been found that the brain's emotional circuitry matures and becomes more balanced with age. In short, the aging brain maintains great capacity and potential, even with the normal episodes of "senior moments."

The following suggestions from the Alliance for Aging Research summarize actions we can take to maintain a healthy brain:

#1 Nourish your noggin: Eat a brain healthy diet
#2 Use it or lose it: Stay mentally active
#3 Work out for your wits: Exercise and keep fit
#4 Interact with others: Stay social
#5 Rest for restoration: Get plenty of sleep

#6 Unwind for your mind: Manage your stress

#7 Guard your gray matter: Protect your head

#8 Think overall health: Control other conditions

#9 Give your brain a break: Avoid unhealthy habits

#10 Understand your risk: Consider your genes

The second question of "will my money last?" requires a highly in-dividualized response. There is not a shortage of people who want to help you answer this question. Most older adults are constantly bombarded with mail, email, and phone invitations from financial planners, investment counselors, insurance salespeople, attorneys, and others to help you protect and maintain your retirement nest egg, if you have one. While financial health is important, it should not be the source of stress and anxiety as we age. For followers of Jesus Christ it begs the question of where our faith and security lie. In this study we will look at scripture that addresses this question.

YOUR TAKE

Read and answer each of the following questions. Discuss your response with your group.

1. Which of the following activities do you do on a regular basis?

___ Walk a mile or more at least 3 times a week

___ Do crossword puzzles, Sudoku. or other puzzles several times a week

___ Eat enough fruits and vegetables every day

___ Learn something new at least once a week

___ Smoke a pack or more of cigarettes a day

___ Exercise at least 3 times a week

___ Continue to gain weight because of your eating habits

___ Get regular check ups

___ Get a minimum of 7 hours sleep each night

___ Drink alcohol in moderation or not at all

___ Drink more than 3 cups of coffee each day

___ Have a healthy social life and good friendships

2. When thinking about supporting yourself as you age, which of the following statements best expresses your feelings and response?

___ I'd better win the lottery.

___ I think I have it figured out.

___ I think I will need to continue working.

___ I've been planning, saving, and investing for a long time; I think I'll be OK..

___ I'd better get a big inheritance or I might be in trouble.

___ I am planning on lowering my lifestyle and overhead and will be OK.

___ I not sure what I am doing and it scares me.

___ Other _____.

YOUR REFLECTION
Read the following passages from the Bible and answer the questions that follow.

Do you not know that your bodies are temples of the Holy Spirit, who is in you, whom you have received from God? You are not your own; you were bought at a price. Therefore honor God with your bodies.
—1 Corinthians 6:19-20

1. Why do you think the apostle Paul equates our bodies with God's temple?

2. Why should we and how can we honor God with the way we treat our bodies?

Do you not know that in a race all the runners run, but only one gets the prize? Run in such a way as to get the prize. Everyone who competes in the games goes into strict training. They do it to get a crown that will not last, but we do it to get a crown that will last forever. Therefore I do not run like someone running aimlessly; I do not fight like a boxer beating the air. No, I strike a blow to my body and make it my slave so that after I have preached to others, I myself will not be disqualified for the prize.
—*Corinthians 9:24-27*

3. What role does self-discipline play in a maturing relationship with Jesus Christ? Have you found self-discipline to be harder or easier as you age?

Therefore I tell you, do not worry about your life, what you will eat or drink; or about your body, what you will wear. Is not life more than food, and the body more than clothes? Look at the birds of the air; they do not sow or reap or store away in barns, and yet your heavenly Father feeds them. Are you not much more valuable than they? Can any one of you by worrying add a single hour to your life?

And why do you worry about clothes? See how the flowers of the field grow. They do not labor or spin. Yet I tell you that not even Solomon in all his splendor was dressed like one of these. If that is how God clothes the grass of the field, which is here today and tomorrow is thrown into the fire, will he not much more clothe you—you of little faith? So do not worry, saying, 'What shall we eat?' or 'What shall we drink?' or 'What shall we wear?' For the pagans run after all these things, and your heavenly Father knows that you need them. But seek first his kingdom and his righteousness, and all these things will be given to you as well. Therefore do not worry about tomorrow, for tomorrow will worry about itself. Each day has enough trouble of its own.
—*Matthew 6:25-34*

4. When it comes to supporting yourself, and perhaps others, are these words of Jesus Christ realistic or unrealistic? Please explain your response.

5. It is common to worry about finances as we age. What is Jesus saying to us about worry in these verses?

6. Has your faith impacted the way you handle your finances? If so, please give some examples.

YOUR APPLICATION

During the coming week, do the following exercises to help you age better both physically and financially.

1. Write down three ways you can do a better job of taking care of your body, the temple of the Holy Spirit. Make these activities practical and doable. Build in accountability, such as doing the activity with someone else. (Examples: eating 2 more portions of fruits and vegetables per day; walking a mile at least 3 times a week; reducing or eliminating a bad habit, such as smoking, etc.)

2. Assess and write down your current financial situation. Determine where changes can be made to retire debt, save more, invest better, increase income, budget better, etc. That is, given your current financial situation, how can you improve your financial health in the next year; 5 years; 10 years? (Factor in contributions to the work of God's kingdom.)

3. Write down the areas you worry about the most, such as health, finances, family, etc. Pray for each of these areas daily. Ask God to reduce your worry and increase your faith in his provisions.

SESSION 5 | HEALTHY AGING 2: EMOTIONALLY

INTRODUCTION
Have one or more group members read the introduction aloud.

The Issue: As we age, how can we stay emotionally healthy?

Research studies have shown that, as we age, emotional and mental health is closely related to physical vitality. It has been shown that regular physical activity can protect and improve our emotional health. In addition, good social relationships with friends, family, and the greater community also contribute to good emotional health in our later years. So too does challenging our brain on a daily basis with new ideas and activities.

The stereotype of aging adults becoming grumpy old men and women has not been supported by recent research. Basically, if you are a negative, grouchy person when you were younger, chances are good that you will be the same or worse as an older adult. Recent studies on the positivity effect have found that older adults are more likely than the young to pay attention to positive stimuli. In short, most of us have a good chance of not becoming cantankerous, crabby old people.

Yet, aging can be a minefield of conflicting emotional ups and downs. Here are a few situations that can produce these ups and downs: becoming empty nesters; divorce; birth of a grandchild; loss of a job; retirement; marriage of your child; caring for parents, children or grandchildren; more leisure time; lack of purpose; illness; work demands; travel; paying off your mortgage; loss of a friend or family member and many more emotional experiences.

Mental health professionals can give us a laundry list of ways we can manage our emotions as we age: get regular physical activity; get enough sleep; maintain good social and family relationships; stimulate your brain with new challenges; don't smoke; use alcohol moderately, if at all; reduce stress; practice relaxation; practice positive thinking; have a good sense of humor; be loving and friendly.

While these certainly constitute good advice, for followers of Jesus Christ there is more.

The Bible clearly states that our emotional health and well-being are directly tied to our relationship with God. Central to our relationship with God is love. Scripture states that God is love; that God so loved the world that he sent his only son; that we are to love the Lord our God and our neighbor as ourselves; and even love our enemies. Love is central to the Christian lifestyle. Consequently healthy emotions flow from God, who is love. As we age as Christians, a deepening relationship with God will help us to live out the healthy emotions he intended.

YOUR TAKE

Read and respond to the following questions. Discuss your responses with your group.

1. Which of the following statements best expresses how you view your emotional life?

___ I am the same person emotionally that I was at 25 years of age.

___ I now have less to get emotional about.

___ I am now more emotionally fragile than I used to be.

___ I find that I cry more easily than ever before.

___ I find that my range of emotions has widened.

___ I find that my range of emotions has narrowed.

___ I am more emotionally healthy than I have ever been.

___ I think emotions are overrated.

___ I am uncomfortable showing my emotions.

___ I think my emotions are an important part of who I am.

___ Other _____.

2. What role do you think emotions play in the Christian life?

___ Emotions are a sign of spiritual weakness.

___ Since we are made in God's image, God must be emotional.

___ Emotions take us deeper in our understanding of God.

___ Jesus Christ was emotional on many occasions and we need to learn from him.

___ In the Bible emotions were shown to be both positive and negative. We need to learn the difference.

___ Emotions are God-given. We need to learn to use them properly to further his kingdom.

___ Other _____.

YOUR REFLECTION

Read the following passages from the Bible and answer the questions that follow.

Rejoice in the Lord always. I will say it again: Rejoice! Let your gentleness be evident to all. The Lord is near. Do not be anxious about anything, but in every situation, by prayer and petition, with thanksgiving, present your requests to God. And the peace of God, which transcends all understanding, will guard your hearts and your minds in Christ Jesus.

Finally, brothers and sisters, whatever is true, whatever is noble, whatever is right, whatever is pure, whatever is lovely, whatever is admirable—if anything is excellent or praiseworthy—think about such things. Whatever you have learned or received or heard from me, or seen in me—put it into practice. And the God of peace will be with you.
—Philippians 4:4-9

1. Does rejoicing and aging seem incompatible to you? If so, why? If not, why not?

2. What is the source of your greatest anxiety? What remedy do these verses give for anxiety?

3. What role does thanksgiving play in dealing with anxiety?

4. Have you ever experienced the peace of God which transcends all understanding? If so, what were the circumstances?

5. What do you think is the relationship between thinking (about whatever is true, noble, right, pure, lovely, admirable, excellent, and praiseworthy) and emotional health and peace?

YOUR APPLICATION

During the coming week do the following exercises to help you move toward greater emotional health.

1. Write down the names of people and things that bring you joy. Spend some time every day thanking God for them.

2. Write down the names of people and things that cause you anxiety. Spend some time every day asking God to give you peace over them.

SESSION 6 | HEALTHY AGING 3: SPIRITUALLY

INTRODUCTION
Have one or more group members read the introduction aloud.

The Issue: As we age, how can we grow spiritually?

Spirituality has changed significantly over the last 50 years. Prior to the 1960s, when we spoke of spirituality, we usually meant Christian spirituality. All that changed in the 1960s. Since then the term *spirituality* embraces a wide range of human experience from a personal relationship with Jesus Christ to weird extraterrestrial experiences. Modern spiritual leaders like the Dalai Lama, Deepak Chopra, and even Oprah, have given the world a spirituality of mix-and-match insights that wander far and wide. Over the past decades best selling books like *The Celestine Prophecy, The DaVinci Code, The Power of Now,* and *The Shack* have offered us unorthodox ways of viewing spirituality. Today, the result is that many people embrace a make-it-up-as-you-go-along spirituality, if they have a spiritual life at all.

For followers of Jesus Christ spirituality is different and hasn't changed for centuries. Yet many ministries today are confused about how to grow people spiritually. Recently, a spiritual formation movement, lead by Richard Foster, Dallas Willard, Ruth Haley Barton, and others, has emphasized the need for Christians to actively pursue spiritual transformation.

But what is spiritual formation or transformation? Dallas Willard writes "Spiritual formation in the tradition of Jesus Christ is the process of transformation of the inmost dimension of the human being, the heart, which is the same as the spirit or will. It is being formed (really, transformed) in such a way that its natural expression comes to be the deeds of Christ done in the power of Christ."

As we age, do we become more spiritual? Research seems to indicate that we do. It seems logical that as we experience loss and face the reality of our mortality, we think more about life after death. Rather than waiting for a deathbed conversion, many people begin or intensify their spiritual search earlier. As we age Christians should take advantage of increased opportunities to enter into spiritual discussions and pursue spiritual growth.

But how do we do spiritual formation? In 2 Peter 1: 3-8 we get a succinct description of the progression of spiritual formation or transformation.

His divine power has given us everything we need for a godly life through our knowledge of him who called us by his own glory and goodness. Through these he has given us his very great and precious promises, so that through them you may participate in the divine nature, having escaped the corruption in the world caused by evil desires.

For this very reason, make every effort to add to your faith goodness; and to goodness, knowledge; and to knowledge, self-control; and to self-control, perseverance; and to perseverance, godliness; and to godliness, mutual affection; and to mutual affection, love. For if you possess these qualities in increasing measure, they will keep you from being ineffective and unproductive in your knowledge of our Lord Jesus Christ.

YOUR TAKE
Read and respond to the following questions. Discuss your responses with your group.

1. On a scale of 0 to 10, where 0 = no importance and 10 = all important, how important is your spiritual life to you?

0   1   2   3   4   5   6   7   8   9   10

No importance   All important

2. Which of the following statements best describes the current state of your spiritual life?

___ I currently have no spiritual life.

___ Spirituality has always confused me, so I can't answer the question.

___ I have been working hard to mature spiritually.

___ I have always felt good about my spiritual life.

___ I feel closer to Jesus Christ than I ever have.

___ I am moving two steps forward and one step back in my spiritual life.

___ I talk to God as often as I can; prayer is central to my spiritual life.

___ Reading and meditating on scripture is central to my spiritual life.

___ I have a spiritual director who helps me grow spiritually.

___ Talking to friends and family helps me grow spiritually.

___ Going to church helps me grow spiritually.

___ Other _____.

YOUR REFLECTION

Read the following passages from the Bible and answer the questions that follow.

So Christ himself gave the apostles, the prophets, the evangelists, the pastors and teachers, to equip his people for works of service, so that the body of Christ may be built up until we all reach unity in the faith and in the knowledge of the Son of God and become mature, attaining to the whole measure of the fullness of Christ.

Then we will no longer be infants, tossed back and forth by the waves, and blown here and there by every wind of teaching and by the cunning and craftiness of people in their deceitful scheming. Instead,

*speaking the truth in love, we will grow to become in every respect
the mature body of him who is the head, that is, Christ. From him the
whole body, joined and held together by every supporting ligament,
grows and builds itself up in love, as each part does its work.*
—*Ephesians 4: 11-16*

1. According to these verses, what are the roles of spiritual leaders in the church (the body of Christ)? Are the spiritual leaders you
know fulfilling these roles? If so, how?

2. What relationship do works of service have to unity in the body
of Christ?

3. According to these verses, how do we become mature followers
of Jesus?

4. What are the consequences of staying as an immature Christian?

5. What does it mean to "speak the truth in love?" What relationship
does it have to spiritual maturity?

6. Why is the metaphor of the human body a good description of the church (body of Christ)? In what positive ways have you experienced other parts of the body ministering to you?

YOUR APPLICATION

During the coming week read and think about the following scripture verses and quotes. Jot down your thoughts and reflect on them throughout the week and beyond.

For this very reason, make every effort to add to your faith goodness; and to goodness, knowledge; and to knowledge, self-control; and to self-control, perseverance; and to perseverance, godliness; and to godliness, mutual affection; and to mutual affection, love. For if you possess these qualities in increasing measure, they will keep you from being ineffective and unproductive in your knowledge of our Lord Jesus Christ.
—2 Peter 1: 5-8

"The world can no longer be left to mere diplomats, politicians, and business leaders. They have done the best they could, no doubt. But this is an age for spiritual heroes- a time for men and women to be heroic in their faith and in spiritual character and power. The greatest danger to the Christian church today is that of pitching its message too low."
—Dallas Willard, The Spirit of the Disciplines : Understanding How God Changes Lives

When I was a child, I talked like a child, I thought like a child, I reasoned like a child. When I became a man, I put the ways of childhood behind me.
—Corinthians 13: 11

"The desperate need today is not for a greater number of intelligent people, or gifted people, but for deep people."
—Richard J. Foster, *Celebration of Discipline: The Path to Spiritual Growth*

But the fruit of the Spirit is love, joy, peace, forbearance, kindness, goodness, faithfulness, gentleness and self-control.
—*Galatians 5: 22-23*

"The purpose of journeying together in spiritual friendship and spiritual community (whether there are just two of you or whether you are in a small group) is to listen to one another's desire for God, to nurture that desire in each other and to support one another in seeking a way of life that is consistent with that desire."
—Ruth Haley Barton, *Sacred Rhythms: Arranging Our Lives for Spiritual Transformation*

Jesus Prays for All Believers
My prayer is not for them alone. I pray also for those who will believe in me through their message, that all of them may be one, Father, just as you are in me and I am in you. May they also be in us so that the world may believe that you have sent me. I have given them the glory that you gave me, that they may be one as we are one— I in them and you in me—so that they may be brought to complete unity. Then the world will know that you sent me and have loved them even as you have loved me.
—*John 17: 20-23*

FURTHER READING

A Long Bright Future by Laura Cartensen

The Longevity Revolution: The Benefits and Challenges of Living a Long Life by Robert N. Butler

Denial of Aging by Muriel R. Gillick

Aging and Ministry in the 21ˢᵗ Century: An Inquiry Approach by Richard H. Gentzler

Living with Purpose in a Worn-Out Body: Spiritual Encouragement for Older Adults by Missy Buchanan

A Vision for the Aging Church: Renewing Ministry for and by Seniors by James M. Houston and Michael Parker

ABOUT THE AUTHOR

Peter Menconi has written and presented widely on generational and aging issues. His rich background as a dentist, pastor, counselor, business owner, conference speaker, husband, father, and grandfather brings unique perspectives to his writing.

Born and raised in Chicago, Pete graduated from the University of Illinois, College of Dentistry and practiced dentistry for 23 years in private practice, in the U.S. Army and in a mission hospital in Kenya, East Africa. In addition, Pete has a M.S. in Counseling Psychology and several years of seminary training. He has also been a commodity futures floor trader, a speaker with the American Dental Association, and a broker of medical and dental practices.

For over 20 years Pete was the outreach pastor at a large church in suburban Denver, Colorado. Currently, he is the president of Mt. Sage Publishing and board member with the CASA Network.

Pete's writings include the book *The Intergenerational Church: Understanding Congregations from WWII to www.com*, The Support Group Series, a 9-book Bible study series, and numerous articles.

Pete and his wife Jean live in the Denver area and they are the parents of 3 adult children and the grandparents of 9 grandchildren.

Pete Menconi can be reached at petermenconi@msn.com.

CASA NETWORK

AGING WELL

BIBLESTUDYSERIES

Finally, a Bible study series for everyone 50 and over who wants to stay in the game as long as possible!

THE AGING CHALLENGE

The primary purpose of this Bible study is to help you take a fresh look at aging, reevaluate your current situation, and consider making some changes.

THE NEW R & R: RETIRED AND REWIRED

The primary purpose of this Bible study is to help you to take a fresh look at retirement, reevaluate your current situation, and consider making some changes.

GENERATIONS TOGETHER

The primary purpose of this Bible study is to help you to take a fresh look at our current generations, how the generations relate, and how we can be better together.